Poetic Dwellings

A Soul's Journey

Helga Vroom

Poetic Dwellings

A Soul's Journey

ELYSSAR PRESS
REDLANDS, CA

Copyright © 2020 by Helga Vroom

All rights reserved. This book or any portion thereof may not be reproduced or used in any manner whatsoever without the express written permission of the publisher except for the use of brief quotations in a book review.

Printed in the United States of America

First Printing, 2020

ISBN 978-1-7334529-1-5

Elyssar Press
175 Bellevue Ave
Redlands, CA 92373

www.ElyssarPress.com

Cover Illustration Painting Copyright by Harry Menne
Cover design by Katia Hage
Book design and production by Stephanie Aoun

Editing by Jessica Yowell and Samar Hage
Photographs by Harry Menne and Dr. Fran Grace
Paintings by Harry Menne

To Duane, Krissie, Dillan and Tanner,

"Just as the wave cannot exist for itself, but must always participate in the swell of the ocean, so we can never experience life by ourselves, but must always share the experience of life that takes place all around us."

— Albert Schweitzer

Preface

All my life, I have enjoyed writing: essays, book reports, opinions, letters, and my journal for my grandchildren. In my late senior years, poetry writing opened up a new meaningful door, which has given me much joy and quite often a lot of healing.

In the beginning, there is the thought process. As the thoughts are being organized, feelings and the unconscious mind kick in. Those avenues travel and are crafted into a precise short form. Few words should express a lot of meaning. In turn each line stirs additional ideas and thoughts.

English is and will always be my second language. In the end, the meaning of the poem is what counts.

Contents

Memories   1

Thoughts   33

Nature   59

Pearls of Wisdom   89

Biography   107

Acknowledgements   108

Memories

"And by the way, everything in life is "writable" about if you have the outgoing guts to do it, and the imagination to improvise. The worst enemy to creativity is self-doubt."

— Silvia Plath

Kitchen table

a seed from mother tree-blanketed by the warm earth
nurtured from sun and rain
grew into a tall, straight tree
overlooking its beautiful homeland

one day
with a painful deafening saw
the tree died

its second life began
as a kitchen table
for happy parents
and their first-born son

time went by
and years did fly
now the big, round table in the nook
can fill a huge, big book
with stories of joy and tears
spanning over many years

a day around the table, once a tree
good morning kisses for you and me
hear the growling tummies
waiting for breakfast with the "Funnies"
one more coffee, please!
but hold off with that morning sneeze
time goes by so quick
leaving for work-can't I play sick?

time went by
and the years did fly
more siblings, laughter, noise, work
and joys thereafter

where did the growing family gather?
in a circle, side by side
locking eyes and feeling loved
problems discussed and solved
and stories told
mother sewing, children doing homework and crafts
receiving friends
all gathering on that beloved table

soon lights get turned off
a quiet house
where everyone sleeps
there stands our table, all by itself
just the moon looking in

years went by
and time did fly
birthdays, holidays, weddings and funerals
the last word spoken—always around our kitchen table

time goes by
the years still fly
the children now grown
flew out of the nest
I sit by myself and rest
with the silent glow of a candle
smiling

hummingbirds
having their fill and all that is close
in a vase, a red rose
to complete the circle of bliss and peace
J. S. Bach's music for my table and me

Newborn

a miracle
my first born
perfect
velvety skin
hair like silk

my hands embrace
this beautiful child
asleep on mother's breast

feeling the little heart beat
incomparable

love and peace
bond
mother and child
with our creator
above

New baby

a new baby
does not ask
to be born

it is a mother's priority
and responsibility
for a 24-hour cycle
to provide for a baby's needs
from the womb
into the world
a huge change

baby needs to be held
spoken to and smiled at
add singing for
an extra plus
when restless
baby needs to be
held and rocked
breastfeeding has
a dual purpose
the most nourishing
and held heart to heart
when walking outside
with baby in a sling
they love the motion and
being close to mom's body
this plus all that fresh air
puts the baby asleep very fast

babies grow up quickly
we need to be aware
of baby's growing needs
playing with other children
story time
singing, talking, and reading
picture books
getting to know
more loving people
and the world around them

if providing well
we have a happy baby
it's the greatest gift
and blessing
a mother could
wish for

Blue

the sky on a
cloudless day
a blue which takes
my breath away

the oceans
roaring waves
their depth
the darkest blue

the flowers
star shaped
bell shaped
smiling faces

the bluebird
brilliant
tweeting
on a branch

the artist's brush
with all the blues
soft, dramatic
in multishades

a fountain pen
in my hand
blue ink
words of love

My Byron

the best Christmas ever
my youngest son
born December 24, 1962
my Christmas angel
my little miracle boy
sharing your birthday with Jesus
perfect from head to toe
a mother's dream
holding you gently
close to my body
sharing the warmth
feeling your heartbeat
the rhythm of life
my hands moving softly
over your velvety skin
and silken hair
not wanting to stop
a gift from heaven
I will be there for you
with all my love
my precious boy
born with a tooth

you came as my angel
and left as my angel
October 28, 1996
life lived and loved
now gone

love lives on forever

Childhood dreams

childhood dreams
a constant thing
dreaming the same dream
over and over again
until puberty came along

I was the only person
on this planet
who could fly
just by myself
how?
by running fast
faster and faster
airborne, spreading arms
stretching head and neck
gaining height
achieving the desired altitude
tilting arms
creating curves
floating smoothly
seeing the world
way up high
with all its beauty
mountains and valleys
rivers, oceans
tiny people
here and there
exhilarating
when landing

people flocked
in great numbers
wishing to learn
how to fly
I failed in my teaching
and remained the only person
who could fly

I just loved my flying dream

Our childhood jobs

our first childhood job
was created by our father
he taught us gardening
he allowed each one of us
a piece of land
about six yards in diameter

we planted herbs and vegetables
from tiny seeds
it was a lot of fun
to observe the growth

after the harvest
herbs and vegetables
were sold to our mother
to prepare the meals

our sole income then was
saved in a little box

when Christmas came along
our earned money
was spent to buy materials
for crafting our presents
which were then given
to our family and relatives

with great anticipation
we looked forward
to Christmas

at last the day arrived and
our little faces radiated with
pride and joy

Two of my earliest childhood memories

waking up in my crib
during the middle of the night
I saw a ghost coming
through the open window
dressed in a flowing gown
in my parents' bedroom
where my crib was placed
I was not scared
I also remember
I was less than three years old
at daylight as I woke up
the ghost was still there
but now I knew, the ghost in form
of my mom's evening gown
placed on a hanger
in the open window frame
the wind playing tricks
with my mom's evening gown
hanging there airing out
after coming home with dad
from the opera or concert
did I have at that moment
a smile on my face?
that I don't remember

I was put down
for my afternoon nap
in my crib
sleep never came

my young mind obsessed
with a painting on the wall
next to my crib
by the famous romantic painter
Phyllip Otto Runge from the 18th century
this painting fascinated me
three young siblings entertained me
the youngest sitting in a wagon
pulled by the two older ones
one of them lifting one arm
indicating "let's go"
there were sunflowers to the left
and a house to the right
both connected by a fence
remembering this painting
kept my young mind occupied
day by day
months perhaps years

now at 89
reading the art section
of my weekly German paper
there it was!!
my childhood painting from
Phyllip Otto Runge
born on an isle
raised with eleven siblings
in the old town of Usedom
in the Baltic Sea

Love

the greatest gift is love

love for your child
love for your parents
love for a friend
love for a sweetheart
love of an animal for the young
love for your country

the love for good things in life

nature
music
books
travel
people
adventure
hiking
communication
and many more
when blessed with love, life is good

my golden rule-the more love one gives, the more love one receives

Did it really happen?

Crystal Cove State Park
hiking South to North
on the Southern California Coast
leaves a memory of a lifetime
endless waves in rhythm
sounding like a crescendo
in a symphonic concert
rock formations crafted
over millions of years
stones with delicate fine lines
smoothed by the waves
tumbling back and forth
seabirds getting their fill
with each step rolling heel to toe
feeling the wet sand
made me a part of the beach
hours passed
coming back
waiting for the "WALK" sign
to cross the Pacific Highway
time to zip open
my fanny pack
to fetch my keys
oh no! keys gone
what's next?
call my children in Hawaii?
no other choice
kind souls
sending their friend to fetch me
and my spare keys
meaning 162 miles round trip
loving kindness in its truest for

the next day
back home again
L.A. Fitness for my swim
need to replace my lost membership keycard
"that's not necessary," they said
"it has been shipped"
I stood motionless—-mouth open
"you mean my keys were found?"
"yes, they searched for the owner
and location of your membership
all the keys were mailed"
smiling and jumping for joy
beaming like lightning in the sky
did it really happen?
yes, it did
an act of true kindness
from a stranger to me
abundantly blessed

Flying

no more standing
no more waiting
no more baggage
no more checking in
now sitting
with anticipation
roaring engines
taking off
gaining altitude
a new world
unfolding with
new perspectives
sandy coastline
waves crashing
endless ocean
glued to the sight
mind and soul
engulfed
all is perfect
oh… let it last

Two firsts while crossing the Atlantic

the first time
at the age of seventeen
leaving Germany
for one year
to study in Bakersfield
my parents and I
drove to Bremerhafen
on the Northern Sea
to board
the SS Neptunia
on her first maiden voyage

hours rushing
climbing on board
horn sounding
ready to sail
waving
till parents
were tiny dots

arms dropping
here I am
goodbyes are sad
joyful what's ahead

fascinated by the
white cliffs of Dover
England's coastline
where my great uncle
Dr. Robert Daniels
spent time in gruesome prison
in the nineteenth century

during Karl Marx's time
for practicing humanity
treating the poor
with no pay
admired by Karl Marx
not accepted by the Germans
it was a different time

the fourth day
violent weather
sea sickness everywhere
including stewardesses
loud speaker pleads
for helping hands
lucky me
feeling fine
ending up
feeding, burping
cuddling and bathing
three infants
for four days
I managed

happy to help
no one knows
when help is needed
and what life expects
from us

my contribution
made my first
more meaningful

You

you went with me
everywhere
across the globe
along the shores
up the ladder of
snowcapped mountains
and desert summits too
kept me safe
and comfortable

YOU

my hiking boots

Taking a cruise

twelve or more stories high
thousands of cruisers
enjoy being pampered
gourmet food
dressed up, or casual
dancing or watching movies
playing crazy games
swimming or walking
playing cards, or reading
loud music
lectures, comedy
guessing games
and much more

part of deck twelve
an island of peace
called "Serenity"
you must be over twenty-one
to choose a lounge or cabana
with a circular view
read, write, sleep, relax
take a walk in the shade or the sun
or watch the world go by and
find the YOU
which had been hidden
until now

Traveling

traveling to faraway lands
a longtime passion
have come to a halt
but my thoughts
bring back
treasured memories
familiar lands
oceans and mountains
various climate zones
cultures and people
where I left part of me

now time moves on
memories of joy and adventures
still much alive
leaving the window
wide open

January first 2017

the air is clear and cool
the wind is a gentle breeze
the sun penetrates through clouds
creating a glitter
over the vast calm ocean
the baby waves fold gently
the only sound there is
sounds of nature
always peaceful
never disturbing
sitting on the sand
very still
body, mind, and soul
restored
refreshed
renewed
I smile

Christmas 2018
7:00 in the morning

black dramatic clouds
rain fell during the night
my plan to start with a walk
on Christmas morning
with Charlotte and Koa
her new two-year old Doberman
seemed to be a great idea
the air was invigorating
pushing mountains of fallen leaves
forward with our feet
the outdoors belonged
to the three of us
wow, what a revitalizing way
to start Christmas morning
the time came
to turn around
right then, the sky opened
endless buckets of rain descending
upon us and mother Earth
downhill intersections turned
into roaring rivers
Koa took rescue under an
extended patio cover of
a parked motorhome
"come on Koa"

we made it back home
soaked
greeted by a rainbow
of spectacular colors
and sunny skies

never to be forgotten

New Year 2019

the sun shines golden red
layers of fog like a feather bed

I go outside dressed in my coat
to start the new year on a high note

ready, give myself a test
turn everyday into its best

not to worry, all will be fine
no long goodbyes for what lie behind

keep downsizing my mind
it cleanses my soul; my face will shine

in any case, little bits are still in me
let go!!!- - -fulfillment it shall be

Valentine's day

born in the U.S.
spreading
and celebrated globally

the flower business
and chocolate industry
thriving

giving presents
meaning human kindness
but let's not forget
the true meaning
of a valentine is
spreading love

that's what the kids
in primary school do

I remember my sons
and years later, my grandsons
came home from school
with smiling eyes
sharing a whole pile
of valentine hearts
from every student
in their class
they truly felt loved
and their demeanor
radiated happiness

one year my youngest grandson
designed his mother's valentine card
and wrote

thank you, mommy
for my toy people
my little dinosaurs
my soccer ball
my this, my that

and on and on it went

I asked Tanner

"if you had no toys
would you still love your mother?"

"yes, I always would love my mommy"
not more was said

when his valentine's card
was completed
Tanner had added

if I had no toys
I would always love you the best

years after that
Tanner's mother mentioned
that valentine's card quite often
with a happy smile

the impact of love lives on

Wishes for the New Year

a little more peace, and less fears
a little more kindness, let the envy freeze
a little more love, much less hate
a little more truth would be great

instead of restlessness, a bit more quietness
instead of "I", a bit more of "YOU"
instead of fear, a bit more courage

strength to handle life, then we will all thrive
problems in sight, search for a light
put the wants behind, seek nature
and beauty you'll find
plant flowers in your garden
before they're put on your grave by the warden

Thoughts

"Compassion is an act of tolerance where kindness and forgiveness reign. When we make the compassionate choice, we enhance the dignity of each individual which is the very essence of Loving them."

—Leo Buscaglia

Surprise

a gift from my friend
a bulb resting in its bed,
which flower might it be?
"time will tell," she said, "you'll see"

day by day, I watched it grow
"you grow fast, not slow"
I measured the stem once a week
12 inches, 24 inches- - -a miracle I see

next morning, not 1, not 2, but 3
brilliant red flowers
hard to believe
magic and beauty, nature holds
a big surprise, joy unfolds

Magnolia is my name
put me out in the rain

Phases of Swimming

Freestyle
Rendezvous in a Pool

standing at the edge of the pool
letting one's body down into water cool
the skin wakes up
water becomes lover's touch
swimming fast
let it last
the crescendo of water's touch
from feet to head above
smooth, swift, and light
water and body unite

Backstroke
Spiritual Endeavor

rolling over and facing the sky
grateful am I that my soul can fly
swimming along
filled with a song
the sky deep blue
clouds dancing only a few
I moved out of life's cage
no baggage at this stage
and learned to die
while much alive

Joy

the feeling
when swimming
water smooth and clear
body light like flying
endless energy
follow nature's element
water and body unite

My day to day

Morning

6 am waking up
slept eight hours
feel half my age
stretching and relaxing
blessed

Pain

ouch
not now
go away
take a deep breath
keep going

Book

reading a good book
the best escape to my nook
it's fascinating
and ever stimulating
the time is mine—moon can shine

Table

around our table
celebrations with loved ones
smiling happy faces
festive setting, tasty food
smiles with good conversation

Humorous travels

a lady tourist
from the U.S.
to Germany, she went
for the Winterfest

weather cold and rainy
when making plans
that wasn't brainy

soon our lady caught a cold
exactly that, she was foretold
now it's too late
being miserable and without a mate

feeling lonely as can be
she does not speak German, you see
one day she took off for the Winterfest
not looking her very best

she crossed the busy street
where cars and pedestrians meet
an officer in the center stood
directing them as best as he could

the lady started sneezing
almost lost her breathing
the officer shouted
"GESUNDHEIT" with a smile
everybody heard that within a mile

what happened next
became the best
"ENGLISH YOU SPEAK,
THAT'S WHAT I SEEK"

she opened up her arms
and hugged the officer
with all her charms

Night rest

a busy day
tired
time for bed
eyes closed
____still awake
what now?
breathe yoga
____still awake
take a walk
on the patio
then sit
let the night speak to me
soft cool winds
embrace my skin
stars above flicker
planes go by

green trees
dressed in black
back to bed
it feels good
____still awake
try visualization
beach
roaring waves
wet sand
endless
____still awake
____still awake

mountains
rich earth
rocks small and tall
intoxicating fresh air
sleeping animals
stillness everywhere
___still awake
my hometown garden
recalling the names
of every flower
blooming in spring
when I was a child

Mother, is that you?

The gift

selecting a gift
for someone special
is a noble act
the giver is driven
by kindness, friendship and love
the gift is lovingly wrapped
anticipating the moment
with stretched out arms
handing the gift to the recipient
"this is for you"
eye contact, soft smiles and
silence
with eager hands
unwrapping the gift
ah-----
then lifting the head
with a grateful smile and happy eyes
"thank you, I love it, how kind of you"
ending in each other's arms
both the recipient and the giver
are blessed with joy and love

Revelation

I hear :"you are thirty years behind"
right you are

content the way I live my life
I look for beauty around me
in nature and people
following my passions and wonders
I don't care to be caught
in the fast track
popularities
riches
I seek peace around me
pray for peace
my belief is rooted in this quote
of Henry Thoreau
"I went to the woods that I might live deliberately
and not come to the end of my life and find
that I had not lived at all"

How These Lines Came to Be Written

waking up
grab water in a cup
swimsuit I slip
oh, another zip
L.A. Fitness I drive
now I am alive
jump in the pool
AAAAAAH, that feels cool
I swim
every day 1 mile
suits me fine
shower then home
tummy growls a bass tone
AAAAAAH, food
so good
candle on the table
food for soul says the label

what time is it?
cannot forget it
yoga at nine
would not miss it
rain or shine
life is just fine
if I only could find more time

once a week, my scrabble group
before I leave, I have some soup
and reading, more reading
my passion rather than weeding

every Thursday, my friends and I hike
everybody says " That's what we like"
four hours of yoga is a must
if not, my body will rust

not to forget my second home
University of Redlands I phone
get time for lectures, discussions and more
soul and brain food galore

my creative writing classes are so much fun
we learn a lot from each other but now I must run
quite often I run out of time
so what!!! A busy life is truly fine

Doors

the subject of doors
is endless
majestic doors
of European castles
and cathedrals
come into my mind
telling stories of
war and peace
kings and queens
the history of their countries
doors to European
opera houses
never forgotten
stepping through doors
of museums
seeing ancient objects
humans held
in their hands
thousands of years ago
admiring the art
of painters and sculptors
makes us speechless
doors of little alpine huts
where the tired hiker
finds protection and rest
when traveling, friendly strangers
open their doors for us
the doors to hospitals and funeral homes
entered and exited with joy or desperation

visualize doors made of
wood, glass, or steel
painted and carved
and the fairy tale doors
when our children's imagination
was exploding
I wonder
is there a museum of doors in our world?

Benches

the bench
on the patio
on the balcony
of the 55th floor
in the city square
in the park
on top of
the summit
benches everywhere
on planet Earth
people of all
walks of life and all ages
speaking different tongues
sitting on benches
smiling, talking, crying
and smiling again
loving, hugging, and kissing
expressing feelings
of life lived
discussing
daily happenings
books
travel and adventures
goals and passions
sharing advice
resting together or
all by themselves
thinking, eyes scanning
maybe people watching

or meditating with
a clear mind and soul
eyes closed
saying the daily prayer
counting all the blessings
of one's life

Tiles

tiles have been around
for centuries

tiles to walk on
for children to run upon
we kneel to pray
and clean up

babies carried
coffins leaving
dancing when
celebrating

tears when loved ones leave
embraces when returning
we put furniture on tiles
tables to eat, write, work, talk and play

we keep guest books
who walks in
and out

tiles are there
for generations
if they could only
tell their stories

Some books

some books merit
a second read
especially when temperatures
climb over hundred
one title was
"Werke und Leben"
"Composition and Life"
of Ludwig van Beethoven
Beethoven was raised in
a dysfunctional family
his complex personality
drove him to learn and compose
becoming the genius in the
world of classical music
it all began in 1781
started composing
when he turned eleven
my mind is traveling back
when I was eleven
following my mother's footsteps
enrolling in my hometown's
conservatory to study piano
across from our home
lived Mr. Neubauer
a minister and
brilliant piano player
time and again
I tiptoed unnoticed
to his fence and listened

for uncountable hours
to the Beethoven sonatas
he played brilliantly
his technique was flawless
with his soul woven among the notes
the famous Waldstein sonata
named after a Count and
one of beethoven's countless promoters
yes, that melody pops up in my mind
right now after 79 years
and another favorite
of mine, "the Moonlight Sonata"
these two and others
belonged to my
repertoire as well
there I stood
listening and listening
not wanting to be
discovered
if someone came along
on this quiet street
I would pretend to find
what I had lost
nothing lost

just found
the heavenly music
with mind and soul of
Ludwig van Beethoven

Hands

ten fingers
the busiest
most versatile
amazing tools
our body has

newborn hands
uncontrollable
such precious sight

soon they learn
eating and drinking
arranging objects
drawing and writing
ready for a lifetime

studying hands
reveals a life's story

hands of a musician
strong yet delicate
hands of an orchestra conductor
very powerful
indicates *pianissimo* and *forte*
rhythms and pauses

thousands of art galleries
all over our globe
exhibit paintings
sculptures and more
all created by gifted hands

scientists, surgeons
architects, and photographers
hands for mankind

sign language for the deaf
fingers express opinions
thumbs up or down
four fingers become a heart

hands are livelihood
of farmers and trade people
for the captain on board
with his crew
the pilot flying
from a continent to another

love expressed
by holding hands
hugging and caressing
tenderly
shaking hands
when connecting
or departing

folding ten fingers
bowing heads
when praying
like in the painting
the Praying Hands
by the famous German painter
Albrecht Duerer

Eyes

eyes like a window
open our world
they speak without words
store in our soul
what is seen and felt

eyes have no boundaries
like sky and oceans
when eye to eye
connect
stories are told instantly

eyes like raindrops
on the window
with tears of joy
and sadness
never to be forgotten

eyes are beautiful
when they think of love
love for family and friends
nature and animals
and all what is beautiful

The 21st century

everywhere
on the street
on the bus
in the stores
and parks
eating a meal
yes, everywhere
young, old, and in between
heads bending
trained fingers racing
touching bottoms
reaching someone
who knows where?
not missing an iota
what's coming on the screen
obsessed
that's what I see
wherever I go
in this digital world
the meaning mindful
is unknown
like observation
and perception
conversation
not practiced
eye contact
and smiles
gone
not even
becoming aware
what took only
a second
someone ripping-off
their pride possession

I am a robot

I am a robot
a black ghost
feeling safe
my heart is made
of metal
let me say
dying will not happen
to me
I only see
all the mistakes
people have made
and everyone has claimed
it was not me
who made the mistakes
then who is the guilty one?

not important anymore
all people died
without people
no more guilt
I, the robot, lives on forever
while the earth
changes its face
looking like the moon

I have said it all
I will wait till the end
till birds
will sing again
and new trees are growing

One thing is for sure
I will never die

Nature

photo by Fran Grace

"There is only one question: how to love the world. Around me the trees stir in their leaves and call out, stay a while. Where does the temple begin and where does it end?
Instructions for living a life:
PAY ATTENTION. BE ASTONISHED. TELL ABOUT."

— MARY OLIVER

The elements
(English version of Die Natur)

the clouds drift
in the firmament
and protect people
on planet Earth
like a blanket
covers the sleeping child

the sun behind
the wall of clouds
seems
gone forever

the clouds become
darker and heavier
any moment
they burst open
and rain covers
earth and oceans

the wind howls louder
the meadows have waves
like the tides in the ocean
ah—let it rain
the growth outdoors
will not stand still

when the morning
waits in front of our door
the sun will shine
thus warming us and
mother Earth

Die Natur

die Wolken wandern im Firmament
und beschuetzen die Menschen auf der Welt
wie eine Decke das schlafende Kind

die Sonne hinter der Wolkenwand
als ob sie fuer immer verschwand

die Wolken werden dunkel und schwer
im nu platzen sie, und Regen prasselt auf Erd und Meer

der Wind faengt an zu toben
die Wiesen haben Wellen wie im Meer die Wogen
wann hoert's wohl auf da Oben?

ach, lass es regnen so viel es will
dann steht das Wachstum der Natur nicht still

wenn der Morgen kommt herbei- - - - glaub mir- - - -
die Sonne strahlt waermend herein

Nature

(I wrote this poem when I was a child in Germany. This is the translation)

I want the wind
in my face
while running,
the sensation
becomes magnified

I want the rain
in my face
mouth open
tongue stretched out
delicious

I want the snow
all over me,
body covered
stars so soft
smiling face

the sky
black clouds
wind howling
trees bending respectfully
homeward I run

Spring

Spring is the awakening
of our planet Earth

there is nothing more beautiful
than to observe how trees dress up
with the tender coat
of fragile light green leaves
the buds on the fruit trees pop
into multicolored flowers
leaving an intoxicating scent
in the air
on the rich moist earth
baby flowers
cannot wait to unfold
their floral smiling faces
the air fills with
a one of a kind, powerful aroma
this is the time
when young and old
seek the outdoors
the garden, the mountains
the seashore, the valleys
letting it all in with deep breathing
and eyes wide open
animals who mated
tend with parental love
to their tiny offspring
surrounded by all this beauty
feeling the joy for life

the love for our creation
the sky, sun, clouds, and rain
tweeting birds with a
heavenly song in the air
let us hope
that this beautiful season
turns people to practice more
loving kindness

Spring break

take a cruise
people on board
mostly seniors

take a cruise
at spring break
mostly children
grandma and grandpa
only here and there

children interact
making friends
trying new activities
bursting with energy
playing, running, laughing
being very happy

mealtime
parents eat lobster
also smoked tongue
children eat hot dogs, pizza
hamburgers, and fries
how can they look so healthy
having endless energy
on all that junk food?

seniors observing children
brings back
long time memories
with big smiles

Summer poetry
[haiku]

sunflower tall straight
nature's art of smiling face
giving joy and awe

lizards love the sun
running up and down the wall
when disturbed they run

baby's face all smiles
both hands reaching for love
legs kicking fast up high

the outdoors helps me
to depart from life's set path
and expected role

[cinquain]

bird
small, mighty
feeding blossom's nectar
relentless
territorial

ocean
wet sand
crashing huge waves
pelicans flying above
meditating

beach
finding treasures
shells all sizes
stones with symmetrical patterns
awesome

rose
velvety red
breathe in the scent
perfection
gift

[triplet]

A two-year-old
sitting on the pot
PLUMP, PLUMP, happy eyes and a big smile

[tonka]

within our known world
in nature one exits the
mainstream to enter
a new world, finding inner
self and reason for living

Summer at 8:00 pm

almost every night at 8:00 pm
during summer time
I sit outside
clear my mind
open my soul to nature
breathe deep and slow
in and out, in and out
feeling the gentle breeze
caress my skin
almost as a lover's touch
a second best
trees feel it too
and moving branches
telling me they do
time does not exist
the evening star
huge, bright, and glittering
takes its journey
along the western sky
on astronomy's time
observing how
the star traveled
from the left side of a palm
to the right side of another
in the time I have been out there

all is peaceful and complete
I allow myself to be drawn
into the world of wonder

feeling grateful and blessed
breathing deep and slow
in and out, in and out

might it be bedtime?
time was not on my mind

no!!!! —— one and a half hours?
it can't be

yes, it was
keep on traveling you beautiful evening star

Yellow

summer time 6:00 am
a fragile line
of golden yellow light
on the horizon

growing bigger then rounder
unfolding into
a yellow golden ball
the sun

lighting planet Earth
one time zone at a time
promising life for all
people, animals and nature

we would not exist without this
astronomical wonder
neither would planet Earth
as we see it

one day at a time
the sun is reflected
in yellow burgeoning
flowers everywhere

gazanias, buttercups, lantanas
tulips, roses, Palo Verde trees
dressed up with hundreds
of little yellow flowers

there she skips the little girl
dancing with a smile
her yellow dress
waving with the wind

and on cold winter nights
spooning up a yellow
soup of squash
before bedtime

then stepping into the night
there it is
the soft glowing yellow
moon

fifty years ago, September 15, 1969
Neil Armstrong landed on the
moon which looked to him like
the California desert

standing on planet Earth
our golden yellow moon
radiates peace
and harmony
good night golden yellow moon

The first rain

my eyes mesmerized
by the rain
a steady downpour
creating puddles
each drop
leaving rings
in motion

a rain dance
turns me
into a dreamer
wrapped up
in a warm blanket
with
the urge
to take a walk
and feel, hear, and look at
the rain
to visualize
nature reviving

that is a special treat

Wild animals' uniqueness

GIRAFFE
with a circular view
in command how true

ELEPHANT
his skin is thick
best defense is his trick

FROG
the ability to jump
to find what he wants

OWL
growing old and wise
being hidden in disguise

TURTLE
never loses his cool
taking time to rule

CHIPMUNK
being frugal, modest, satisfied
his eating habits rectified

LADYBUG
meaning luck never harm
people call me their charm

Bird free

the beginning
was a cozy nest
protected and safe
nurtured by
Mama and Papa bird
my siblings and I
my family
fed from morning
till night
growing strong
who'll be the first
to fly out of the nest?
we all tried to be the one

it happened fast
we were ready
a bit nervous and unsure
and suddenly
the nest was empty
one, two, three
the world was ours
free to explore
looking for safe landings
taking off again
soon we made it
from tree to tree
to the rich earth
where food was in abundance

other birds abound
some smaller
some bigger
some dressed up
in rainbow colors
tweeting melodiously
we all grew strong and fit

our migration vacation at last
what a thrill
the oceans and mountains
to be stored into our bird brain
till one day
all of us
found our mates
starting the same cycle
all over again

Dogs

the eyes of a dog
beautiful, loving, and peaceful
like those of a child
having been loved

dogs are devoted
to their family
eager to interpret
commands

dogs are protective of
master and surroundings
intelligent to sense
oncoming dangers

dogs detecting the demeanor
in people, also
new diseases
not discovered by us
dogs in groups
at the dog park
get along famously
running and playing

dogs should be
role models for people
we would have a better world
if we learned from them
THE MEANING OF KINDNESS AND LOVE and more

Love

like oxygen
essential
creates
the smile of life
sustains

brings out the best
connects people
creates helping
hands

builds survivors
heals all animals
builds peace
on planet Earth

connects us all
what is good
what is beautiful

No price tag

beauty of nature
magic
wildflowers
brilliant colors
along the trails
also filling beds
creeping uphill
meditate on a bluebell
brings smiles and joy
to our soul and
heals a wounded heart
all different shades of green
everywhere
the pine trees
stretching in perfection
unbelievable symmetry
ah! the scent
close eyes and breathe
oak trees have their
own mind which
way to grow
providing shade
for the tired hiker
above the endless
blue sky
clouds all shapes
wandering
let it shine
let it rain

let it storm
beauty, drama, and joy
everywhere
all free

tomorrow
we wander
endless beaches
all free

The color blue

outdoors we find the deepest blues
open your eyes, it is true

the deep blue sky of a cloudless day
we will often find in the month of May

the bluest lake in our USA
Crater lake, because of its depth they say

famous painters use blue to paint
van Gogh's blue lilies pure like saints

blue flowers are my favorite kind
bluebell bushes in my front yard you'll find

the blossoms of a laughing face
as delicate as grandma's lace

the blue ocean I am very fond
when swimming, body and water bond

and last, but not least
wrapped in a blue blanket, my little baby boy
with bright blue eyes
what a joy

Reflections - Outdoors

the outdoors help me
to depart from life's
prescribed path
and the expected role
of being appropriate

in nature, I exit
the mainstream
entering a new world
within our world

finding my true self
and the reason for living

I give thanks
to the universe for the light
the sun for its warmth
the elements for power and energy
the beauty of nature
the privilege to be here
the blessings which embrace me
today we climbed one more
ladder of the earth

The summit of San Gorgonio mountain

I stand alone
clouds surround me
on this lonely majestic mountain
swimming in the fog
like an island in the ocean

quiet soul
my heart fills
with God's creation
below lies the world of
worries, money, broken souls

freedom
I find here

And this is how it started

long time ago, a tiny little seed fell to the ground
it landed on the rich, moist forest floor
millions of years of natural decay
had turned the bed of earth into compost

and it stayed there, the little speck of seed, unnoticed
but little by little, the seed sprouted into a tree
nurtured by rain, warmed by the sun, sheltered in the ground
asleep under the snow

spring time came, and the little tree woke up
spring storms howled upon it
so young, but very flexible, it just danced back and forth
when summer came, it grew taller, bigger, and stronger

and now, when the storms race thru the forest
branches and leaves touch
the crown of the tree moves back and forth
sounding like a beautiful melody, playing the song of the forest
when you hear it once, you will never forget

if the tree could tell a story, might it be like this
"I am the host of many bird families
I am the home for chipmunks
I am the freeway for millions of ants
I am the playground for children to hide and seek
while the woodpeckers play the drums."

one day when the tree matured, its life changed
deafening noises came upon the tree- - -and the tree was cut down
but sadness turned into great joy
the beautiful tree turned into a table

A table for a family with children and their friends

Everyone who came into their house
couldn't believe how beautiful it was
It felt so smooth, it was so shiny
the colors were deep brown with lines and circles
And best of all, it was there forever
and as years went by, it too had
a story to tell

One---two---three

there she was
all by herself
dressed in
a loose garment
her hat for
protection
walking trails
up and down
mountains
canyons
coastlines
around lakes
and meadows
carpeted with flowers
in brilliant rainbow colors
listening to the
soft winds
dancing for
billions of years
moving clouds
in the atmosphere
of planet Earth
the beauty of nature is
a priceless gift
for a lifetime

[AROUND THE BEND]
came along her twin
walking together
in silence
feeling connected
by nature's beauty
no word spoken

[ANOTHER BEND]

the trio was completed
dressed the same
in hiker's comfort
walking together
in silence
feeling connected
by nature's beauty
no word spoken

Blooming Desert

with more of the winter rain
the desert is spectacular
cacti blooming in deep purple colors
groundcover in yellows, whites and pinks
a delicate carpet

that's the time to hike
camp overnight
let the beauty
become part of us

quiet soul
listen to the gentle breeze
the sounds of nature

eyes wide open
near and far
skyline with summits
clouds drifting

in awe

Pearls of Wisdom

"To live in this world, you must be able to do three things: to love what is mortal; to hold it against your bones knowing your own life depends on it;
And when the time comes to let go, to let go."

— MARY OLIVER

Sharing

an open mind
towards learning
new adventures
following passions
gathering wisdom
with friends and
like-minded people
opens new doors
leading in new directions
in new worlds
abundant blessings
become ours

Living joy

life is only
a moment

compare
millions of years

when people lived
before we came along

we are fools
to create problems
which burden and blind us
when we let them
linger on and on

problems will come
solve them and let go

life is full of joys
make them yours

live them day in and day out
sprinkle all joys with love
and laughter

now life is no longer a moment

Life

just as music
is the space
between notes

just as the stars
are beautiful
because of the space
between them

just as the sun
strikes raindrops
at a certain angle
and throws
a prism of color
across the sky

the space where I exist
the middle
it creates something sublime
life- - whatever it is- - is short

Doors of my life

during our lifetime
we enter and exit thousands of doors
many doors have left a lifetime of memories
filled our hearts with joy
love, and learning experiences
sometimes hardships and tears

I crossed the first door
in the loving arms of my mother
leaving the hospital where I was born
growing up racing in baby style on all fours
soon crossing doors from room to room
it did not take long to meet the neighbor
entering their door to welcoming smiles
the doors of special new friends
the huge winged church door
where I was rewarded with beautiful music
then the door to my kindergarten
learning, having fun, making more friends
soon after, the door for
the big kids' school
proudly I belonged to that group
every door in my school unveiled
a new world of learning

then came World War II
the sirens howled and everybody ran
for safety through the heavy door
into the cold basement
there were bunk beds for us kids, but
how could we sleep with bombs exploding?

"where is mom, here she comes"
"what were you doing upstairs?"
"just ironing dad's dress shirts
there will be no electricity after this"

on a certain day of the week
many hours standing in line
in snow and ice
to enter the grocer's door
to get a few rationed staples
or just return home
empty handed

when starting high school
and opening
the doors of higher learning
we were evacuated
to safer grounds
living in hotels with our teachers
doors away from home
a new experience

when I was 17
I traveled by sea and air to
California for a scholarship
doors on the ocean liner
and the plane were firsts for me
from then on, let the reader's
imagination visualize the
thousands of doors I was
privileged to enter, enjoying
and learning much about
life, cultures, and its people

many doors, many choices
each to be considered wisely

my house has a new door
a heavy wooden door with a
little window to open
for my eyes to see
who is coming
"welcome to my home
my friends". and happily
I open
my beautiful door

Wisdoms

Only when we master the art of forgiving do we practice wisdom.

It would be good if we naturally knew how to lean in.

All that we learn comes from the mind and heart. Good breeding comes from living.

In every adventure of joy, we experience the reason for living.

Nothing belongs to us, only the time in which we live. Let's make the most out of it.

The greatest misfortune of the human soul is to lose all enthusiasm.

When we reach the lowest points in our lives, count our many blessings and we become grateful and healed.

If we are unable to travel, why not travel in the books we read. Adventure unfolds.

Seek nature and take a walk. Open your eyes and all is beautiful.

We have to accept life for what it is. Only then, can we hear the unwanted.

We come into the world not only to know it, but we must learn how to improve it.

Nothing is more difficult than to have patience with oneself to carry our own weaknesses.

Nothing makes our world so vast as when we have friends far away.

We all need to honor the path of a friend. Harmony unfolds.

We are connected to soul friends and each one of us can hold up the other.

How beautiful people are when they practice love.

When you love, you are surrounded by light, like the seed which was hidden in the earth that grows towards the sun.

If we have a long way ahead of ourselves, don't run.

Happy memories stay with us and become treasures.

Growing is the feeling, when the infinite beginning leads to eternity.

Reflections

GIFT
everyone of us is unique
we were created with our identity
which is our reality
it is our task
to share this gift

CHANGE
every change is a departure
master it
make room for
what the future holds

DESIRE
desire opens horizons
leading us to hope
so we understand reality
and accept it

GREAT FULLNESS
whatever happens in our life
great fullness
heals and nurtures
everything

HAPPINESS
you can travel endlessly
to find happiness
you will never find it
unless you seek it
in yourself first
be ready
and allow happiness
to come as a surprise

JOY I
put yourself into life's motion
it is everywhere
it surrounds you
just open yourself
feel the awareness
a joy of life

JOY II
fun floats on the surface
joy lives deep in our soul
allowing us
to add wings to fun

JOY III
joy of life is
the art of the moment
to sense life's vibration
live it
become absorbed
and experience total bliss

DESTINY
to take and let go
accept your life's destiny
work at it
draw your own blueprint
and you learn to let go

RESPECT
respect
the weak
the small
the great
respect lifts one's soul
you discover in yourself
what you did not know you had

SADNESS
pick a flower
meditate
feel the surprise

PATIENCE
when I am patient
with myself
and learn to like it
balance returns

On silence

my thoughts are silent
my judgement is silent
my worries are silent
silence surrounds me
I am a free bird

Often, we lose
our inner silence

through meditation
inner silence is restored
our soul enters a sanctuary
we find again
our true self

the sounds in nature
don't disturb silence
they add depth to silence
silence is a healing chamber
for our thoughts

not only our body needs hygiene
our soul does too
there is no better soul hygiene
than silence

we can only achieve true silence
if we put judgment aside

where is the place
where I can express
my feelings
in a healing way?

nature, music, friends, writing

Aging

long time ago
when I was young
aging did not occur
just other people were old
very old indeed

time moved slowly
soon faster and faster
now I am among the "old"
yet senior life is very special

I am blessed with wisdom
I learned to forgive and
practice loving kindness
I am grateful for life and love
family and home
friends my jewels

staying active
my independence
reading and thinking
strength to carry burdens
walking, yoga, and swimming
my eyes still seeing
wrinkles don't matter
the old tree's bark
cracks too
what's within
and how we share that
alone matters

To ponder over

love often will heal
provided the soul is
open to receive
and to return love gracefully

love your neighbor means
to respect his total being

if we live in the present
we discover
with eyes and soul
the vast beauty around us

if we see reality
in the light of love
our soul overflows
with joy

we will only discover real life
if we choose
to seek new adventures
big or small

hurts become scars
learn not to waste
energy on self
instead start living

to go through a door
with a conscience
means to leave

everything behind you
and become open
to the new environment

be aware of your thoughts
practice this exercise
everything starts with a thought
it can be either healing
or destroying

Biography

About the author

Helga Vroom was born in Germany in 1930. Her parents instilled in her a love for classical music, nature, travel, books and more, which she has followed her lifelong as her passions. She came to the United States as a student. The love of writing poems began in 2016 in her senior years. For her, poems are stories of a few words which express a lot - reliving her life, and feeling joy and contentment.

Helga is on YOUTUBE for 3 minutes.

Subject: Yoga, swimming, and senior lifestyle; swam 8,571

Painter and Photographer Harry Menne (1919-2012)

Harry Menne was born in the Dutch East Indies, and grew up on the lush tropical isle of Java with its priceless background of native art, music, dance, and sculpture. He fell in love with the California scenery, especially where it is left untouched by recent civilization.

Mr. Menne always insists on quality in his wide range of subjects from portrait studies to land and seascapes.

Acknowledgments

A big thank you to my friend and publisher Katia Hage, who guided me, and shared her gifted mind. It was truly fun to work with her, and enjoy her sparkling personality with her amazing talents. A million thanks to you for your endless hard work and your creative mind which turned our book into what it has become. Another big thank you to Jessica Yowell and Samar Hage for editing my poetry so brilliantly. Their professional ideas and devotion were immensely appreciated.

www.ingramcontent.com/pod-product-compliance
Lightning Source LLC
Chambersburg PA
CBHW061210070526
44583CB00025B/3187